AGE

of

BEAUTY

Workbook

CASIE KINDL

Cover and interior designs were curated using Canva Pro.
Back cover photo credit to Angela Divine Photography.
Design credit to Stacy Marquardt and Rosin Marketing Solutions.

ISBN (eBook): 978-1-998393-05-2
ISBN (Paperback): 978-1-998393-18-9
ISBN (Hardcover): 978-1-998393-17-6

A.I. Free. Made with love by a Human.

This workbook is dedicated to my amazing children, Carson and Elle.

May the work you are doing not only help you to feel more beautiful, whole and complete, but also make this world a better place for you and for generations to come.

TABLE OF CONTENTS

TABLE OF CONTENTS
CONTINUED

Author's Note

Although you sometimes feel "not-enough" in your life, the truth is you are a beautiful woman, inside and out. You always have been and always will be. You just desire to feel and believe it more, as do I. We are on this journey together. Yes, I wrote this book for you. Yet the truth is, I also needed it for me. Like you, I sometimes feel like an imposter, criticize myself internally, feel anxious, or uncertain about my place at the table.

Then there are times I feel on top of the world, like I can be and do anything I desire. You feel this too, yet want to feel it more often, more completely.

If this is why you're here, then you've landed in the right place. You've landed at the beginning of a path to seeing and understanding yourself more deeply, chapter by chapter. With knowledge and acceptance of where you are currently, you can begin The Shift into the fullness of who you are as a woman. You will move closer to who you want to be in your relationships, in your work and in your life.

Each week, I recommend reading one chapter from the **AGE OF BEAUTY** book, followed by completing the companion exercises in this workbook. You may desire to move faster, but the biggest changes in your life will not happen as you read a chapter or complete exercises in the workbook. Deep and lasting change will happen with lived experience. Through these pages, you will develop an ever-increasing awareness of where you are and where you desire to be. Just please do not rush the process.

This journey requires approximately an hour of your time per week to read a chapter in **AGE OF BEAUTY**, then complete exercises in this companion workbook. All other "work" will happen in your daily life - catching yourself when your inner critic gets too loud to reframe her narrative in a more supportive way - or noticing how judgment may be keeping you stuck.

If you desire to break away from the endless push of the latest beauty and wellness trends in order to be "enough", this workbook will allow you to see, own, and love your beauty within.

You can still enjoy your self-care routines, and feel deeply confident.

Before you jump in, I want to offer you encouragement. This walk will be difficult at times, but you are a strong woman, capable of achieving your desires. You will learn to see yourself more lovingly, feel more youthful, and become more present in your life. Remember you have a tribe of other women, also on this path toward feeling deeply beautiful. You are not alone. You will be guided, supported, and celebrated on the way as we walk this journey together.

I look forward to seeing you in your light!

♡ Casie

INTRODUCTION

Why did you pick up this workbook?

Why now?

You're a busy woman and inevitably, committing yourself to this workbook will take time from something else important in your life. So, why are you really here?

How beautiful do you feel, honestly?

On a scale of 1-10, how do you view the idea of aging?
1 is "I hate birthdays" and 10 is "I'm embracing it fully"

What does the number you chose mean to you?

How do you want to view yourself as you age?

Specifically, how do you want to perceive yourself and your body, through all ages and stages of life?

If you truly believed in fully owning your inner and outer beauty, then how would the below aspects in your life be different? Detail the 'why' for each one.

In your intimate life...

In your career/professional life...

In your social life...

In your family life...

With your physical well-being...

What is getting in the way of you fully owning your beauty today?

How long have you held onto a belief that once X (insert something important) happens, then you will feel more whole and beautiful?

Imagine you have completed the Age of Beauty book and workbook. Envision you have created a whole new way of being in the world. Don't hold back.

Anything is possible for you.

Now state, with intention, how the new you feels and lives your life?

Restate that same intention in the present. For example, if you want to feel better about yourself and your body, state, "I feel loving and self-accepting when I look at myself in the mirror. I radiate confidence when talking with others."

You may not fully believe your intention yet, and that's okay. However, be sure to write your statement as though you are already living this reality.

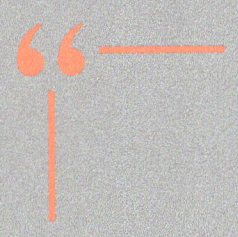

Finally, how do you define beauty?

CHAPTER ONE:
THE TAPESTRY

Chapter One
The Tapestry

What is your earliest memory of unconditional love, freedom and playfulness you experienced as a child?

When you observe a baby or puppy, what feelings or emotions are evoked within you?

What are your spiritual or religious beliefs? What do you resonate with in terms of a higher power or entity beyond the human race?

Chapter One
The Tapestry

Why do you believe you are here? What is your purpose in life?

What is your first memory of feeling disconnected from the unconditional love and acceptance you were born knowing? Perhaps this is a time you changed or hid who you were to fit in, to feel accepted, or to have your needs met.

List other times you received the message that you somehow needed to change yourself in order to be fully accepted or to feel safer.

Chapter One
The Tapestry

How are you currently adjusting yourself to fit into others' expectations of you?

What do you feel inside when you do this?

Chapter One
The Tapestry

How do you define beauty?

When you aren't feeling beautiful, what are your go-to's to feel more aesthetically appealing?

How long does the "good feeling" last?

What does this tell you about your go-to's?

Chapter One
The Tapestry

What habits do you have that are only for your benefit? Focus on the ones that are not based on an expectation of needing to look, be or behave in a certain way for others' benefit.

What body and/or life changes are you currently facing that feel most difficult to accept?

CHAPTER TWO:
THE STRIVING

Chapter Two
The Striving

In what areas of your life are you striving to be more, do better, or be recognized and seen for who you really are?

Pick one to two of the above areas. For each, write down what this striving/hustling feels like to you.

With all of this striving to accomplish what you have, honestly answer:

On a scale of 1-10, how happy are you?

1 = Extremely Unhappy and 10 = Extremely Happy

Chapter Two
The Striving

What "whispers" have you heard or are you hearing that there's another way? That this way of being is no longer working so well for you?

What "bandaids" have you used to avoid feeling this lack or not being enough in your life?

What adaptations have you made to be the accomplished woman you are now?

Chapter Two
The Striving

Who are you blaming in your life for feeling the way you do?

In what areas of your life is your identity and sense of self-worth most connected to an accomplishment you have achieved?

CHAPTER THREE:
THE RESISTANCE

Chapter Three
The Resistance

What is the "equation" you were taught would create happiness, fulfillment and wholeness in your life?

When did you first realize this equation you followed so well wasn't the full answer? When did the realization hit that there was something more, perhaps deeper to be experienced?

Chapter Three
The Resistance

In what ways are you judging yourself?

What judgements do you have toward those you work with? Your family? Your friends?

Where in your life are you comparing yourself to others, or believing there is a "right" or "wrong" way to be, that you are either rockin' or not measuring up to?

Chapter Three
The Resistance

Where do you feel this tension in your body, and how would you describe it?

How long has it been present within you?

What do you wish you could yells screams or say to the world if there were no implications no judgment, and no consequence?

The Resistance

How have you coped with the disconnect between what is really in your heart and mind to share, versus keeping it in as you believe you "should"?

What are the subtle voices within saying about where you are not measuring up in your life?

In what ways have you "armored up" your image, your sense of control or your actions to ignore this subtle voice?

Chapter Three
The Resistance

What area(s) of your life feel difficult or are often a struggle? How long have you been dealing with each of them?

For the struggles that have persisted longer, how would you describe the intensity of them over time?

What information does this provide about that particular area of your life?

Where is your body "crying out"? Perhaps an area of persistent pain/tension or a diagnosis?

Chapter Three
The Resistance

On a scale of 1-10, how would you rate your stress and anxiety levels?
1 is no stress/anxiety, and 10 is debilitating levels; it's hard to function.

And what does that number mean to you?

On a scale of 1-10, how would you rate your resentment, anger or frustration?
1 is nonexistent, and 10 is almost rageful toward certain people/events in my life.

How committed are you to allowing life to continue showing you another way through whispers, yells, and challenges versus practively doing the work?
1 is "I'm staying the course. things are 'fine,'" and 10 is "I'm ready to make whatever change necessary, starting today."

CHAPTER FOUR:
THE RECKONING

Chapter Four
The Reckoning

Where are you showing up in the way you "should" be, even though it feels forced? Meaning, if you could have it your way, you wouldn't even do it.

What are you afraid of happening if you were to show up differently, or not do the things you "should" be doing at work and in your personal life? In other words, what lies below the edge of the metaphorical cliff?

Chapter Four
The Reckoning

When in your life have you felt as though you've hit "rock bottom" or like life has repeatedly smacked you in the face? What did that experience feel like in the moment?

What are your signs to let you know when you are in catabolic/low/negative energy?

What have you been ignoring/avoiding in your life because it feels easier than facing it head-on?

Chapter Four
The Reckoning

Would you generally characterize the resistance/challenges in your life as improving or worsening over time? What does this tell you about yourself and your current situation?

How ready are you to take a leap of faith into the unknown, as a way to feel more beautiful, whole and complete in who you are as a woman?

1 is "I'm good I'm staying in the safety of the known, even though it sucks at times and I don't feel truly, deeply beautiful" and 10 is "When can we start?!"

 ———— ———— ———— ————

CHAPTER FIVE:
THE SHIFT

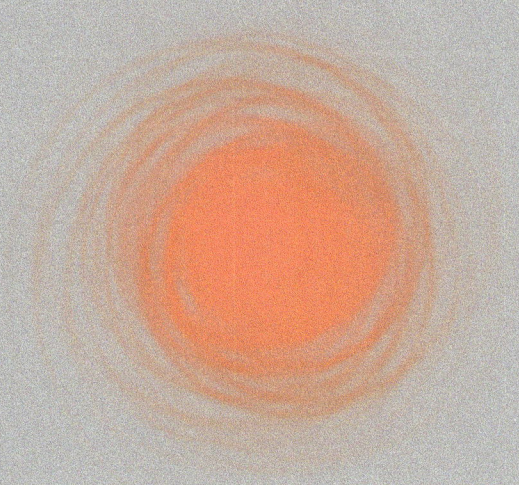

Chapter Five
The Shift

What supports, including therapy, have you considered but not yet pursued?

What is holding you back from pursuing them?

What professionals, services, books, podcasts or other resources have you tried?

The Shift

How did each resource help fuel your sense of inner beauty and confidence?

What other rituals do you maintain that you would like to stay committed to, as they help boost your feeling of beauty and confidence? This can include anything from Botox to meditation or anything else important to your wellbeing.

What clues do you have that you're in the midst of, or ready for a substantial shift in how you perceive yourself and your body?

CHAPTER SIX:
FINDING YOU-TH

Chapter Six

Finding YOU-th

Where do you notice negative thoughts and behaviors in your life?

When those situations occur again, what other ways could you respond to increase your energy instead of feeling angry, drained or defeated?

Where in your life are you already feeling energized or optimistic?

Own your energy.

Finding YOU-th

With your awareness, how could you either lean into this energy more or bring it into other, more challenging areas of your life? Be sure to answer in a way that feels authentic to you. Toxic positivity will not help move you forward.

Where in your personal life can you create more fun?

How about professionally?

Own your energy.

Chapter Six
Finding YOU-th

The level of energy from which you are most often responding attracts what you're currently experiencing in your life.

Looking at what your life could be like at different energy levels allows you to begin to sense you can change the way you are existing.

And once you do that,
you'll be able to choose your life,
instead of having life's experiences
choose you!

-Bruce D. Schneider

Own your energy.

Chapter Six Finding YOU-th

Who have you observed being a "wet blanket"? Perhaps they drain your energy, seem down and out or are not comfortable in their own skin?

Conversely, who do you know or have you seen that has an exciting, vibrant or radiant energy about them?

What is it about the high-vibe person that lets you know, for certain, they are not defined by their age and have a youthful energy to their being?

What will you commit to in order to own your energy in a way that supports you feeling more excited, youthful and energized?

You are not your age.

Chapter Six

Finding YOU-th

What do you really want for yourself and your life?

What decisions are you currently making that feel good, authentic and aligned to your vision?

Conversely, what are you doing that goes against your vision, because you feel an obligation to conform?

Find you

Chapter Six
Finding YOU-th

We so often make decisions based on thoughts in our head, before checking in with our heart or intuition. However, both can be powerful tools in helping you feel more aligned. When can you tell your heart or conscience is trying to tell you something?

When your intuition or gut instinct is pulling you toward a certain path, what feelings do you experience in your body?

What can you do to become more aligned in your head (thoughts), heart (feeling) and gut (instinct)?

Find your

Finding YOU-th

How do you imagine this alignment will help direct you in more authentic decision making?

Instead of trying to fit into the box of expectations from the world, let the world know who you are, and have it fit in around you.
- Law of Being

If you truly embodied this inner belief, what would be different in your life?

Find your

CHAPTER SEVEN: INNER BEAUTY + RADIANCE

Chapter Seven

Inner Beauty + Radiance

How many times have you said, 'I'll be happy when'...?

In the first column below, list some things you believe will make you happy. In the second column, write how you will feel when you gain those things.

What you believe will make you happy	How you'll feel

How many of the things you listed in the first column are actually in your complete control?

Happy girls are the prettiest girls.

Chapter Seven

Inner Beauty + Radiance

What does this exercise mean to you?

What are the sacrifices you are making today in order to create a happier tomorrow?

Is this sacrifice worth it? *Yes / No*

If not, what can you change to create more happiness today, knowing there is no guarantee or promise of tomorrow?

Happy girls are the prettiest girls.

Inner Beauty + Radiance

What is the word you use to describe the deeper essence of someone – the part of them that seems perhaps eternal, timeless or beyond their physical body?

What experience taught you, with certainty, this deeper essence exists in others?

What do you tend to first notice about yourself when you look in the mirror?

What are you committed to doing instead to see the beauty within yourself and your core, spirit or soul within?

Mirror, mirror on the wall...

Chapter Seven

Inner Beauty + Radiance

"We are greater than we appear to be.

One of the most difficult challenges you have in this world is to look past who you see in the mirror to become self-loving and accepting.

Why is this so difficult to do?

Because in order to accept everything you are, you must know, without a doubt, that you are more than your reflection.

Whether you focus on your physical appearance or anything else, as soon as you label yourself, you limit yourself.

You can overcome the powerful illusions of the physical world." – Bruce D. Schneider

To remember this, repeat one of the phrases below a few times to see how it feels.

Look deep into your own eyes, to the window of your soul, and repeat this until you evoke an emotion:

> I am greater than I think I am.

Or you could try repeating the words

> I love you.

Mirror, mirror on the wall...

Inner Beauty + Radiance

What are you most afraid of?

In reality, what is the worst that could happen?

What can you identify within yourself, that you know would step in to help avoid a worst-case scenario from playing out?

Relationship with fear.

Chapter Seven

Inner Beauty + Radiance

Think of a time in your life when you were incredibly fearful, riddled with anxiety and uncertain of what would happen. What did you learn about yourself from the way you got through this difficult situation?

Next time you feel afraid or anxious about what might happen, what can you do instead to remind yourself that you don't have to choose fear? Remember, you can authentically let fear go in exchange for a more supportive thought.

Power of Mind + You = Your Reality
— Law of Being

CHAPTER EIGHT:
FROM WELLNESS TO WHOLENESS

From Wellness to Wholeness

What is one small practice you can commit to daily to raise your vibe? To help you feel joyful and grounded? State this in the present, such as "I dance daily to my favorite song" or "before I get out of bed, I think of three things I'm grateful for, and one I will let go of", etc.

Raise your vibe

Chapter Eight

From Wellness to Wholeness

As you think back on your life, what are some memories that still have an emotional hold on you?

To begin releasing the emotional hold these past events have on you, write down the thoughts and feelings you still have about the situations you recalled.

Reframe your past.

Chapter Eight

From Wellness to Wholeness

What are some possibilities of a new resolution to these old memories?

What do you really want to say now to the people who were there?

What do you want to say to yourself?

Reframe your past.

Chapter Eight

From Wellness to Wholeness

Are your experiences stepping stones or stumbling blocks, and why?

How would changing the way you think about painful experiences affect the way you are living now?

Reframe your past.

Chapter Eight

From Wellness to Wholeness

Choose a resolution to a difficult experience that feels believable to you. Embody this belief fully. Breathe into this new reality. With each deep inhale you take, breathe in the feelings and emotions of the new resolution. On each full exhale, allow the old, more difficult memory to fade away from your being.

What feelings and emotions came up for you as you went through this exercise?

Reframe your past.

Chapter Eight

From Wellness to Wholeness

What are ways you currently support your wholeness that feel good to you in each of the following areas?

Physical:

Emotional:

Spiritual:

Social:

Mental:

Read through this list, and take a moment to celebrate how committed you truly are to your wellbeing. These are no small efforts you have made, and you deserve to be celebrated.

Beyond beauty.

Chapter Eight

From Wellness to Wholeness

In what ways does your pursuit of wellbeing and wholeness feel difficult, forced, or like you are not measuring up in some way?

For each of these, take a moment to turn inward and ask yourself, "What needs to happen in order to feel better about myself here?" Then listen to your inner voice. Write down what comes up in each area.

If the answers feel comforting, clear, or kind, then you can be assured they are coming from your Higher Self. If they still feel a bit shaming, obligatory, or leave you feeling bad in some way, it's likely your inner critic.
That's okay. This approach to wellbeing is a practice.
Continue to ask and tune in with yourself.
Over time, you will come to recognize the more loving inner voice.
That's the one you can choose to listen to.

Beyond beauty.

CHAPTER NINE: CONFIDENCE

Chapter Nine Confidence

When you think back to being "confident" in your past, what images or memories come to mind?

On a scale of 1-10, how fleeting was this confidence?

1 is "It was there one second and gone the next", and 10 is "It was a deep, lasting inner confidence that is still present within me today."

① ——— ③ ——— ⑤ ——— ⑦ ——— ⑩

Grow your confidence.

Chapter Nine
Confidence

What are all the ways your body supports you in enjoying your life, allowing you to do things you love and connect meaningfully with others?

What qualities do you possess to make you uniquely you, that you genuinely appreciate about yourself?

Next time you look in the mirror or catch yourself being critical, what can you do instead to stand in the light of your beauty to feel better about yourself?

Grow your confidence

Chapter Nine
Confidence

What part of your body or physical appearance do you least like?

What would the kindest, most loving person you know say to you about your scar, blemish, or imperfection?

Now, allow yourself to be the kindest person you know and repeat what you wrote above out loud to yourself in the mirror while gazing either at your imperfection or into your own eyes.

Grow your confidence

Confidence

What came up for you as you went through this exercise?

Beauty is in the eyes of the Beholder. You are the beholder.

Grow your confidence.

Chapter Nine
Confidence

"Values, or the principals you live by, are a product of the experiences you've had.

Your family, your religion, and your community all influence your values.

You are driven by your values, yet they may not reflect what you really want out of life.

They may only be the things you were taught that you want."

-Bruce D. Schneider

Understand your value(s).

When going through this list, it is vitally important that you decide whether these values are really important to you and are relevant to your life today, or whether they are someone else's values from the past that no longer define who you are. For each value, rate whether it is:

1 - Extremely important to you
2 - Important to you
3 - Somewhat important to you
4 - Not very important to you
5 - Not important to you at all

	Accountability		Compassion		Fun		Order		Self-Expression
	Achievement		Confidence		Generosity		Parenting		Self-Respect
	Adaptability		Connection		Gratitude		Patience		Sensuality
	Adventure		Courage		Growth		Perseverance		Service
	Authenticity		Creativity		Honesty		Power		Spirituality
	Balance		Curiosity		Humor		Privacy		Success
	Beauty		Environment		Independence		Professionalism		Trust
	Belonging		Fairness		Integrity		Recognition		Truth
	Caring		Family		Joy		Respect		Understanding
	Clarity		Financial Stability		Leadership		Responsibility		Vulnerability
	Collaboration		Forgiveness		Learning		Risk-Taking		Wisdom
	Commitment		Freedom		Love		Security		
	Community		Friendship		Nature		Self-Discipline		

Values list credit to the Institute of Professional Excellence in Coaching

Now, list your top 3-5 values and rank them in order of importance to you.

VALUES
1.
2.
3.
4.
5.

Consider which of these really matter most to you, as opposed to values you think you "should" uphold, then re-write your top values based on any new perspective you've gained.

Rewrite

Understand your value(s).

Chapter Nine

Confidence

Consider an important decision you are trying to make in your life currently. Now, with recognition of what you most value, consider how potential decisions either support or negate each value.

Based on this learning, what decision will you make?

How can you use your knowledge of what you value to make quick and confident decisions in other areas of your life?

Understand your value(s).

Confidence

What are some of the messages your gremlin voice says to you? Remember, this is the voice inside that speaks to your limitations, not your greatness.

What is your earliest memory of this voice showing up in your life?

How could this gremlin voice have been protecting you at the time?

You are not the voice inside your head.

Confidence

How well is this gremlin voice serving you today?

Since this is just a small voice inside that once was trying to protect you but is no longer needed, what would you like to say to the gremlin or have it do for you instead?

You are not the voice inside your head.

When you say this out loud to your gremlin, what do you feel? Keep refining what you say until you come up with something, perhaps a new role, that feels good and allows you to move forward.

Finally, how can you recognize when your inner voice is one of intuition, or your Higher Self versus a gremlin voice?

You are not the voice inside your head.

CHAPTER TEN:
SELF CARE TO SUSTAIN

In what ways have you put others' needs ahead of your own, to your own detriment?

What underlying belief have you carried driving you to do so much for others to the point of feeling exhausted, worn down or resentful?

What is a more supportive thought you could adopt instead?

Chapter Ten
Self Care to Sustain

Find a quiet time and space where you can dedicate ten minutes to writing your future-self journal entry here. You can light a candle, relax your shoulders, listen to Betsy's meditation, brew a cup of tea or do anything else to help center into this space. Remember to write in the present tense, as though you are already living your ideal life.

Future-self journals

Future Self Journal continued...

Chapter Ten
Self Care to Sustain

Let yourself get fully angry or overcome with sadness about what is happening to you. Remember, this is your safe and confidential space to let it all out. Don't hold back. Allow every hateful, hurtful thing to be said in the space below, and allow your mind to spiral as it sometimes does.

Rant for relief.

Rant for relief continued...

What do you feel after having written everything out on the page?

Now, feel free to rip this page out of your notebook and throw it away.

Rant for relief.

Chapter Ten
Self Care to Sustain

Over the course of this next week, what cold-therapy strategy will you try daily?

After your first cold shower, bath or plunge, note here what your predominant thoughts were in the moment.

Continue this practice daily throughout the week.

After your seventh cold-therapy session, note here what thoughts ran through your mind.

How is your energy?
1 is "Nothing has changed.", and 10 is "I feel fully energized and in control of my thoughts, in the shower and in life."

①   ③   ⑤   ⑦   ⑩

Cold shower.

What are a few self-care rituals you will adopt for yourself going forward, that you know are realistic, and you will stay committed to daily?

1.

2.

3.

What will be your quick and easy go-to form of self-care in case of emergency, when you're at your lowest of lows?

CHAPTER ELEVEN: AGE WITH GRACE

Chapter Eleven
Age With Grace

Identify in your mind a past, painful experience. As you recall it, where do you notice tension or restriction in your body?

In your chosen safe space, set a timer for no more than ten minutes. Allow yourself to relax into, and breathe through all the feelings that come up for you around this painful experience. Do this by either relaxing into where you notice restriction in your body, or feeling the pain in "waves" of acceptance and letting go.

What emotions and physical sensations in your body came up for you during the exercise?

What do you feel after having tried integrating and accepting this prior experience?

Integrate pain.

Chapter Eleven
Age With Grace

How old are you chronologically?

Biologically?

Emotionally?

What are your beliefs around an ongoing, everlasting part of you that lives on, beyond this physical form?

Choose your age.

How might this exercise change the way you think about aging?

Next time you are asked your age, how will you respond?

What will you do differently, or how will you act differently to help influence your age, either emotionally, biologically or spiritually?

Choose your age.

Chapter Eleven
Age With Grace

What words or phrases do you use when talking about your health?

What physical pain or health concerns are you currently facing?

What relationship might you see between the language you use and your current state of health?

Health.

Age With Grace

How might your thoughts, language, or habits have contributed to creating or maintaining your physical symptoms?

Notice where you feel symptoms in your body, then breathe into and feel that part of your body. After a few deep breaths, ask yourself if your pain/body part could speak, what would it say? What do your physical symptoms have to tell you? Then sit quietly for a reply.

What ideas or awareness came to you, if any?

Health.

Chapter Eleven
Age With Grace

What is going well for you physically, in your body and with your health?

What do you genuinely appreciate about your current state of health?

How will you talk about and focus upon what you currently appreciate about your health, to create even greater wellbeing in your life?

Health

CHAPTER TWELVE: BECOMING TIMELESS

Chapter Twelve
Becoming Timeless

Identify some common thoughts that run through your mind on a daily or weekly basis. List them here.

Chapter Twelve
Becoming Timeless

Now, let's categorize each thought into past, present or future thought.

PAST	PRESENT	FUTURE

Presence.

Chapter Twelve
Becoming Timeless

When you catch yourself out of the present moment, what will you do to bring yourself back to the here and now?

Remember that your power rests in the present moment.
When you find your mind is in the past or future,
gently note it, take a deep breath, and
bring yourself back into the joy of what surrounds you.
-Law of Being

Chapter Twelve
Becoming Timeless

Return to Chapter 9 to recall your top values. Make any adjustments as needed and list them below in column 1.

In column 2, list all the things that light you up, bring you joy, or you lose track of time doing.

In column 3, consider all you're naturally good at or have been recognized for. Feel free to call a best friend to get more insight into this one.

Don't hold back on this exercise. Let all of your ideas come pouring out.

What I Value	What I Love	What I Am Good At

Be on purpose.

Chapter Twelve
Becoming Timeless

After spending some time reviewing your list, what new ideas come to mind for things you could be doing to live closer to your purpose?

Remember, this can be anything in your personal or professional life.

Be on purpose

Chapter Twelve
Becoming Timeless

What do you do for fun? For no other reason than to enjoy yourself?

What are the things that make you happiest? What brings you the most joy and laughter? What allows you to feel most free and child-like?

How will you create more of this good-vibe energy in your life?

Be a kd.

Chapter Twelve
Becoming Timeless

In what ways do you attempt to control, or not fully trust, your body?

What can you do instead to re-learn how to trust yourself and your body to work for and not against you?

How will you deepen your spirituality, to move closer to the timeless quality already within you?

Be a kid.

CHAPTER THIRTEEN: FULFILLMENT AND HAPPINESS

Fulfillment and Happiness

How would you rate your default state?

1 is "I can always find a reason to be cynical and judgmental.", and 10 is "No matter what comes my way, I know I can choose to be happy."

What in your life is already bringing you joy and happiness that you could focus on to create more of?

What good do you see in yourself and others?

What can you do to begin believing better days are ahead for you instead of waiting for the other shoe to drop?

Becoming happier.

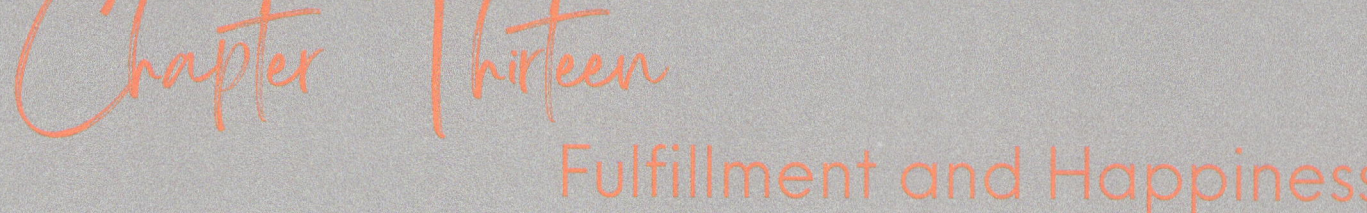

Chapter Thirteen
Fulfillment and Happiness

Look back to the table you completed in Chapter 7 of this workbook to note the feelings you hope to experience once you achieve certain milestones in your life.

Once you're able to identify those feelings listed in column two, then what?

And then what would happen?

What underlying feelings would you be experiencing?

What are additional ways you can create these same desired feelings in your life now?

Love is all you need.

Chapter Thirteen

Fulfillment and Happiness

 Know you can weather your moods.

What does your inner gremlin voice sound like when you're in a downward spiral?

Next time you're spiraling downward in negative self talk, what will you do to catch yourself and authentically bring yourself back up?

What if you embodied the belief that no one cares or notices much of what you're doing, other than you?

Smile and laugh, and don't take yourself or life too seriously.

Five keys.

Chapter Thirteen

Fulfillment and Happiness

 Choose balance without judgment.

In what ways do you feel guilty or judge yourself when you are taking time to refuel?

Where do you notice this unease in your body? What does it feel like?

Going forward, when you take time for self-care, how will you nurture yourself instead of falling into this old pattern of accompanying guilt?

Five keys.

Chapter Thirteen
Fulfillment and Happiness

 Develop support systems.

Consider the people you spend the most time with, and then note whether they predominantly gain or drain your energy.

People

DRAIN	GAIN

Five keys.

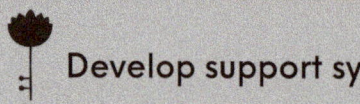
Develop support systems.

After reviewing this list, note who in your life has your back no matter what, and what specifically you appreciate about them.

Consider reaching out to someone you identified on this list, to let them know what they mean to you and why.

Five keys.

Chapter Thirteen
Fulfillment and Happiness

 Challenge yourself to grow.

In what ways do you continue to grow in your personal and professional life?

Revisit your purpose identified in Chapter 12, then consider ways you can lean into or learn more about the things that light you up.

Five keys.

Chapter Thirteen

Fulfillment and Happiness

 Define yourself and express your gifts.

In the space below, describe your favorite version of you. How does she feel? Who is she being in the world? What does she get to celebrate? How does she love? How does she live?

What is one thing you can borrow from your favorite self to live closer to her today?

Is it more important to you to be right or to be happy?

CHAPTER FOURTEEN:
THE RISING

Chapter Fourteen
The Rising

Map out in the space below the woman you are rising to become, from this day forward. Declare the richness of her life, her experiences, and her support system. Consider how she finally gets to feel.

Rise for you

Chapter Fourteen
The Rising

As your commitment to yourself to rise into the woman you are becoming, you can trust that when you feel good, you are on the right path.

When you fall off, what will you do to realign yourself? How will you remember the Truth of who you are, as a beautiful, rising woman, who is human and will make mistakes, but stays committed to the journey?

Rise for you.

Chapter Fourteen
The Rising

What part of the life of a flower do you most identify with currently?

What lessons from the life of a flower will you take forward to remind yourself of your beauty at every stage, your ability to be present or the journey of being born anew?

How will you remember this Truth about yourself when life gets tough?

Rise like a flower.

Chapter Fourteen
The Rising

How do you make decisions currently?

1 is "Decisions leave me unsettled, wondering if I made the 'right' choice.", and 10 is "I can make a decision calmly and confidently, trust it was the best decision and then move on."

① ------- ③ ------- ⑤ ------- ⑦ ------- ⑩

List some decisions you make everyday, and indicate whether you are making the choice based on love or fear. For example, if you choose to exercise: do you do so because you are nurturing and caring for your body (love), or are you doing so because you feel you should or have to, in order to be accepted (fear).

LOVE	FEAR

Love over fear.

Chapter Fourteen
The Rising

How will you lean more into love
while making important decisions in your life?

Love over fear.

CHAPTER FIFTEEN: INTEGRATE AND ACCEPT

Chapter Fifteen

Integrate and Accept

What joy, wonder, beautiful experiences and love have you brought into your life already?

In what ways did your past self come up short? For each shortcoming, how can you forgive her for these missteps?

Do you believe she was doing the best she knew how at the time?

Yes / No

Chapter Fifteen

Integrate and Accept

Close your eyes and imagine that your past, younger self is sitting with you. As you envision her, share silently or out loud how much you love and appreciate her.

What came up for you during this exercise?

Chapter Fifteen

Integrate and Accept

Think of a time you judged someone this week. After judging them, either out loud or to yourself, what did you feel later in the day?

List the top three things you still judge about yourself.

1.
2.
3.

Forgive for your future.

Chapter Fifteen

Integrate and Accept

For each, remember back to the circumstances that surrounded you at the time. What might have been causing stress in your life and what knowledge (or lack thereof) did you have at the time?

Considering this, do you believe you were doing the best you knew how at the time?

Is that worthy of your forgiveness?

Yes / No

Forgive for your future.

Chapter Fifteen

Integrate and Accept

If you still haven't forgiven yourself fully for past mistakes, that's okay. However, I invite you to return to seeing this younger version of yourself sitting alongside you.

Close your eyes, take a few deep breaths, and do whatever you need to do to feel comfortable and connected to her in this quiet space.

When you are ready, let her know how you better see and understand her, and you will continue to learn to forgive. If you are at the point of offering genuine forgiveness, let her know how you have forgiven her and why.

What came up for you in going through this practice?

Forgive for your future

Chapter Fifteen

Integrate and Accept

Through this journey, what are you learning about your parents or others who may have hurt you that you would like to now forgive?

Feel free, if the exercise of sitting with your past self felt impactful to you, to do the same with others you want to forgive or let them know how much you appreciate them, and why. Take your time with these exercises. If anything triggering comes forward that you are unable to release, be sure to seek the guidance of a licensed therapist.

Forgive for your future.

Chapter Fifteen

Integrate and Accept

Think of the person you most judge in your life and list below the ways in which you judge them.

Take two or three of the above judgments you make (there is no shame in this, as we all do it) and consider how you may wish you could act in this same way but don't feel you should. Or think back to a time when you too were behaving in a similar way to what you don't like/judge in them.

After identifying these patterns, if you feel called, envision them now sitting next to you in your quiet space. With eyes closed, you can practice seeing them. Share how you too have behaved like them, perhaps forgiving them, and appreciating them for the lessons they brought to you and the resultant growth you experienced.

We forgive to free ourselves. We forgive for our own wellbeing.

the unhappy judge.

CHAPTER SIXTEEN:
FULL CIRCLE

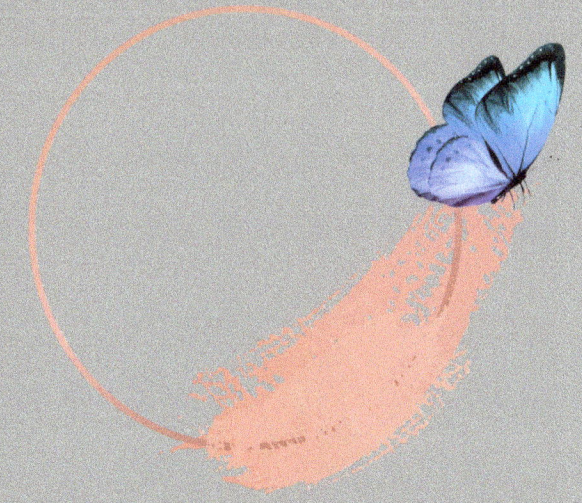

Chapter Sixteen
Full Circle

In your quest for genuine self love, self forgiveness is critical.
To what extent have you forgiven yourself?

1 is "I know I should, but can't.", and 10 is "I love and forgive myself fully."

① —— ③ —— ⑤ —— ⑦ —— ⑩

When have you shared love freely in your life? With whom do you share this gift?

How can you give more of your unlimited resource of love to others?

And yourself?

Chapter Sixteen
Full Circle

Now, write your manifesto for how you will love, see and appreciate your beauty within. Remember to state this in the present.

You are worth it.
You are beautiful.
You are aging.

You are in your
Age of Beauty.

For information about Age of Beauty programs available currently,
connect with me at www.kindlcoaching.com.

I look forward to seeing you in your light.

Notes

Notes

Notes

Acknowledgements

I am immensely grateful to my husband, Dustin, for supporting me on this soul-expressing journey of writing my first book. I could not have done it without your love and tolerance of me in this process.

Thank you to our children, Carson and Elle, for serving as the catalyst to become the woman I am today.

Thank you to Stacy Marquardt, Larissa Soehn with Next Page Publishing and her amazing team, including Ruth Fae and Amy Vogel; the women in Age of Beauty book club: KT Anderson, Kristen Charette, Jenny Oko, Therese Dlugosch, Ruth Johnson; the Modern Well community, Julie Burton, Madison Hewlett, Jasna Burza, Betsy Weiner, the amazing ladies of '23 Mastermind, Connie Greenberg, Breah Ostendorf, Stacy Hartmann, Jason Gracia, my many prior clients who taught me what it means to age beautifully, Angela Divine, and my wonderfully supportive group of friends and family who offered me encouragement along the way.

Thank you.